James Oglethorpe
Discover the Life of a Colonial American

Kieran Walsh

Rourke

Publishing LLC

Vero Beach, Florida 32964

www.rourkepublishing.com

PHOTO CREDITS: Pages 7, 13 ©Getty Images; page 8 Library of Congress; All other photos ©North Wind Picture Archives

Title Page: *A cannon protects Oglethorpe's 1770 settlement on St. Simon's Island.*

Editor: Frank Sloan

Cover and page design by Nicola Stratford

Library of Congress Cataloging-in-Publication Data

Walsh, Kieran.
    James Oglethorpe / Kieran Walsh.
        p. cm. -- (Discover the life of a colonial American)
    Includes bibliographical references and index.
    ISBN 1-59515-138-9
    1. Oglethorpe, James Edward, 1696-1785--Juvenile literature. 2. Georgia--History--Colonial period, ca. 1600-1775--Juvenile literature. 3. Governors--Georgia--Biography--Juvenile literature. I. Title. II. Series: Walsh, Kieran. Discover the life of a colonial American.
    F289.O37W35 2004
    975.8'02'092--dc22

                                                    2004009654

Printed in the USA

CG/CG

Table of Contents

The Young Oglethorpe

James Edward Oglethorpe was born on December 22, 1696, in Essex, England. Oglethorpe grew up in a **military** family. When he was very young, James lost his father and a brother when they left home to fight in a war against France and Spain.

After attending Oxford University, Oglethorpe was made Captain of the Queen's Guard. At this time, he was only 20 years old.

The war for the Spanish succession, in which Oglethorpe's father and brother were killed

A Member of Parliament

Oglethorpe's military experience led to his election to **Parliament**, the British house of **government**, in 1722.

As a member of Parliament, Oglethorpe became concerned with **debtors**. Debtors were people kept in prison because they couldn't pay their bills.

The prisons were usually dirty. Debtors often died in prison from diseases like smallpox.

A debtors' prison in England

A Colony for Debtors

Oglethorpe learned of an idea to create a **penal colony** for debtors in America. The British government liked this idea. This was partly because, at the time, the Spanish controlled Florida. The British hoped that the **establishment** of a colony near Florida would keep the Spanish from taking over.

A **charter** was granted to Oglethorpe and 20 other men to create a new American colony. To honor King George II, Oglethorpe named this area Georgia.

King George II of England

The reason

Oglethorpe chose Savannah was that the swamps there would act as a good natural defense against the Spanish.

Oglethorpe found swamps like these all along the Savannah River.

Oglethorpe in America

Along with 116 settlers, Oglethorpe traveled to America in early 1733. They landed on the shore of South Carolina.

Traveling south, Oglethorpe chose the area of what is now Savannah, Georgia, as the site for the new colony. This land actually belonged to the Indians, but Oglethorpe convinced them to give it up.

Oglethorpe meets Native Americans in 1733.

Building Forts

James Oglethorpe insisted that members of the Georgia colony have military training. With  the threat of the Spanish in the south, Oglethorpe ordered that a number of defensive forts should be built.

Oglethorpe met with the Yamacraw Indians in Georgia.

Because Oglethorpe could be a stern leader, he wasn't popular with everyone. Some of the settlers were particularly angry with Oglethorpe's laws against alcohol and slavery.

Oglethorpe also met with colonists.

Invading Florida

When England declared war on Spain in 1739, Oglethorpe invaded Florida. Fighting during this war was difficult. Many forts that Oglethorpe captured were later recaptured by the Spanish.

Oglethorpe and his men attack the Spanish at St. Augustine.

The Battle of Bloody Marsh

Oglethorpe's greatest victory during this time took place in 1742 at the Battle of Bloody Marsh. In this battle, Oglethorpe and his men defeated a Spanish party much larger than their own.

A view of Savannah around 1740, when the city was founded

The Savanah River

In 1743, Oglethorpe was called back to England to face charges brought against him by one of his own men. These charges were later dropped.

Oglethorpe reads a book.

Signing Over the Charter

Even though Oglethorpe had defended Georgia from the Spanish, many British were unhappy with his leadership style and his war efforts.

Though he continued working as a general for England, Oglethorpe signed over his charter of Georgia to the British government in 1752. He would never again return to the state he had founded.

A Greatly Admired Man

After retiring in 1754, Oglethorpe became a very influential figure. He was greatly admired by important people like John Adams, Samuel Johnson, and Alexander Pope. He died in 1785. Georgia exists today because of the work of James Oglethorpe. Not only did Oglethorpe found Georgia, but he also defended it at a time when it could have been easily invaded.

The remains of the fort at St. Simon's Island

Oglethorpe dressed in military armor

Important Dates to Remember

1696	Born in Essex, England
1716	Made Captain of the Queen's Guard
1722	Elected to Parliament
1733	Establishes debtors' colony in America
1739	England declares war on Spain; Oglethorpe invades Florida
1752	Signs over charter of Georgia to British government
1785	Dies in England

Glossary

charter (CHART ur) — a contract

debtors (DET urz) — people who owe money

defense (DEE FENTS) — protection

establishment (es TAB lish munt) — creation

government (GUV urn munt) — the ruling body of a country

military (MIL uh tar ee) — part of a country's defenses; the armed forces

Parliament (PAR luh munt) — the law-making portion of the British government

penal colony (PEE nul KOL uh nee) — a place where people who have broken the law are sent to live

Index

Further Reading

Girod, Christina M. *The Thirteen Colonies: Georgia*. Lucent, 2001
Lommel, Cookie. *James Oglethorpe, Humanitarian and Soldier*. Chelsea House, 2000
Stefoff, Rebecca. *Colonial Times: 1600-1700*. Benchmark Books, 2001
Stefoff, Rebecca. *Voices from Colonial Life*. Benchmark Books, 2003
Wiener, Roberta. *The Thirteen Colonies: Georgia*. Raintree-Steck Vaughn, 2004

Websites to Visit

http://www.infoplease.com/ce6/people/A0836428.html
Infoplease – James Edward Oglethorpe
http://www.savannahgeorgia.com/   Savannah, Georgia
http://www.parliament.uk/   Parliament

About the Author

Kieran Walsh is a writer of children's nonfiction books, primarily on historical and social studies topics. Walsh has been involved in the children's book field as editor, proofreader, and illustrator as well as author.